pause & reflect

MEDITATIONS FOR CHANGE

T0096510

pause & reflect

MEDITATIONS FOR CHANGE

ONE VOICE
PRESS

EVANSTON, ILLINOIS

One Voice Press
1233 Central St., Evanston, IL 60202

Printed in the United States of America on
acid-free paper ∞

ISBN: 978-1-61851-239-0
26   25   24   23   4   3   2   1

Cover design by Carlos Esparza
Book design by Patrick Falso

CONTENTS

INTRODUCTION

There is much in our modern world competing for our attention. Technology is changing at a pace so rapid that most of us cannot keep up, let alone take the time to process the ways in which it is affecting us. As we go about our daily lives we are seemingly assaulted with an endless series of distractions. The need to retreat from the stress and chaos that so often surrounds us, to center ourselves and reflect on our inner reality, has never been of more vital importance. It is with this in mind that One Voice Press is happy to present this, the fifth title in its *Pause & Reflect* series.

Pause & Reflect is a series that presents meditative passages from the writings of the Bahá'í Faith arranged around particular themes. While the Bahá'í Faith places a great deal of importance on meditation and the cultivation of spirituality, it is also a religion that calls for action and societal transformation. Meditation, from a Bahá'í perspective, is not exclusively a means for personal growth but also a tool that should equip us with insights and awareness that can be translated into action in our lives and in the communities in which we live.

The theme of this volume is *change*. 'Abdu'l-Bahá—one of the Central Figures of the Bahá'í Faith, and considered by Bahá'ís to be the perfect exemplar of the Faith's teachings—stated the following when speaking to an audience in Paris in 1911: "My hope for you is that you will progress in the world of spirit, as well as in the world of matter; that your intelligence will develop, your knowledge will augment, and your understanding be widened. You must ever press forward, never standing still; avoid stagnation, the first step to a backward movement, to decay." His words would seem to apply both to individuals and to the society to which they belong. If we seek, on an individual level, to apply spiritual principles to our lives and to learn, reflect, and grow in the process, our efforts will naturally radiate outward to our families, our neighborhoods, and to the communities of which we are a part. If we accompany one another on this path and seek to apply principles—such as justice, equality, and unity—to our lives and to the life of our community, then social transformation becomes possible.

The sections of this book reflect the Bahá'í perspective that three interconnected protagonists collaborate in this process: the individual, the institutions, and the community. The institutions mentioned in some of the passages refer to Bahá'í institutions tasked with facilitating the growth and well-being of the community. However, whether one is familiar with these institutions or not, the principles and ideas presented in this section can provide guidance for anyone who governs, and they can apply to any collective endeavor aimed at social transformation.

Change can be difficult and even scary. It often involves stepping outside our comfort zone or sacrificing the familiar for something new. But if we wish to grow and move forward in our individual lives and if we wish to address the myriad problems facing our world today, change is necessary. It is hoped that the passages collected here offer some inspiration and some helpful concepts for those wishing to make changes in their lives and transform the world around them.

The Individual

BAHÁ'U'LLÁH

1

Only when the lamp of search, of earnest striving, of longing desire, of passionate devotion, of fervid love, of rapture, and ecstasy, is kindled within the seeker's heart, and the breeze of His loving-kindness is wafted upon his soul, will the darkness of error be dispelled, the mists of doubts and misgivings be dissipated, and the lights of knowledge and certitude envelop his being. At that hour will the Mystic Herald, bearing the joyful tidings of the Spirit, shine forth from the City of God resplendent as the morn, and, through the trumpet-blast of knowledge, will awaken the heart, the soul, and the spirit from the slumber of heedlessness. Then will the manifold favors and outpouring grace of the holy and everlasting Spirit confer such new life upon the seeker that he will find himself endowed with a new eye, a new ear, a new heart, and a new mind. He will contemplate the manifest signs of the universe, and will penetrate the hidden mysteries of the soul. Gazing with the eye of God, he will perceive within every atom a door that leadeth him to the stations of absolute certitude.

He will discover in all things the mysteries of Divine Revelation, and the evidences of an everlasting Manifestation.

2

The Divine Springtime is come, O Most Exalted Pen, for the Festival of the All-Merciful is fast approaching. Bestir thyself, and magnify, before the entire creation, the name of God, and celebrate His praise, in such wise that all created things may be regenerated and made new.

3

Know ye that God will not, in this day, accept your thoughts, nor your remembrance of Him, nor your turning towards Him, nor your devotions, nor your vigilance, unless ye be made new in the estimation of this Servant, could ye but perceive it.

4

O My Servant!
Free thyself from the fetters of this world, and loose thy soul from the prison of self. Seize thy chance, for it will come to thee no more.

5

All that which ye potentially possess can, however, be manifested only as a result of your own volition. Your own acts testify to this truth . . .

6

O people of God! Do not busy yourselves in your own concerns; let your thoughts be fixed upon that which will rehabilitate the fortunes of mankind and sanctify the hearts and souls of men. This can best be achieved through pure and holy deeds, through a virtuous life and a goodly behavior.

7

Strain every nerve to acquire both inner and outer perfections, for the fruit of the human tree hath ever been and will ever be perfections both within and without. It is not desirable that a man be left without knowledge or skills, for he is then but a barren tree. Then, so much as capacity and capability allow, ye needs must deck the tree of being with fruits such as knowledge, wisdom, spiritual perception and eloquent speech.

‘ABDU’L-BAHÁ

8

For you I desire spiritual distinction—that is, you must become eminent and distinguished in morals. In the love of God you must become distinguished from all else. You must become distinguished for loving humanity, for unity and accord, for love and justice. In brief, you must become distinguished in all the virtues of the human world—for faithfulness and sincerity, for justice and fidelity, for firmness and steadfastness, for philanthropic deeds and service to the human world, for love toward every human being, for unity and accord with all people, for removing prejudices and promoting international peace. Finally, you must become distinguished for heavenly illumination and for acquiring the bestowals of God.

9

And the honor and distinction of the individual consist in this, that he among all the world's multitudes should become a source of social good. Is any larger bounty conceivable than this, that an individual, looking within himself, should find that by the confirming grace of God he has become the cause of peace and well-being, of happiness and advantage to his fellow men? No, by the one true God, there is no greater bliss, no more complete delight.

10

My hope for you is that you will progress in the world of spirit, as well as in the world of matter; that your intelligence will develop, your knowledge will augment, and your understanding be widened.

You must ever press forward, never standing still; avoid stagnation, the first step to a backward movement, to decay.

11

Remember not your own limitations; the help of God will come to you. Forget yourself. God's help will surely come!

When you call on the Mercy of God waiting to reinforce you, your strength will be tenfold.

12

Rest assured that the breathings of the Holy Spirit will loosen thy tongue. Speak, therefore; speak out with great courage at every meeting. When thou art about to begin thine address, turn first to Bahá'u'lláh, and ask for the confirmations of the Holy Spirit, then open thy lips and say whatever is suggested to thy heart; this, however, with the utmost courage, dignity and conviction. It is my hope that from day to day your gatherings will grow and flourish, and that those who are seeking after truth will hearken therein to reasoned arguments and conclusive proofs. I am with you heart and soul at every meeting; be sure of this.

13

Strive that your actions day by day may be beautiful prayers. Turn towards God, and seek always to do that which is right and noble. Enrich the poor, raise the fallen, comfort the sorrowful, bring healing to the sick, reassure the fearful, rescue the oppressed, bring hope to the hopeless, shelter the destitute!

14

When you wish to reflect upon or consider a matter, you consult something within you. You say, shall I do it, or shall I not do it? Is it better to make this journey or abandon it? Whom do you consult? Who is within you deciding this question? Surely there is a distinct power, an intelligent ego. Were it not distinct from your ego, you would not be consulting it. It is greater than the faculty of thought. It is your spirit which teaches you, which advises and decides upon matters.

15

In man there are two natures; his spiritual or higher nature and his material or lower nature. In one he approaches God, in the other he lives for the world alone. Signs of both these natures are to be found in men. In his material aspect he expresses untruth, cruelty and injustice; all these are the outcome of his lower nature. The attributes of his Divine nature are shown forth in love, mercy, kindness, truth and justice, one and all being expressions of his higher nature. Every good habit, every noble quality belongs to man's spiritual nature, whereas all his imperfections and sinful actions are born of his material nature.

16

When our thoughts are filled with the bitterness of this world, let us turn our eyes to the sweetness of God's compassion and He will send us heavenly calm!

17

Note thou carefully that in this world of being, all things must ever be made new. Look at the material world about thee, see how it hath now been renewed. The thoughts have changed, the ways of life have been revised, the sciences and arts show a new vigour, discoveries and inventions are new, perceptions are new.

18

A good character is in the sight of God and His chosen ones and the possessors of insight, the most excellent and praiseworthy of all things, but always on condition that its center of emanation should be reason and knowledge and its base should be true moderation.

19

O ye beloved of the Lord! Strive to become the manifestations of the love of God, the lamps of divine guidance shining amongst the kindreds of the earth with the light of love and concord.

20

Character is the true criterion of humanity. Anyone who possesses a good character, who has faith in God and is firm, whose actions are good, whose speech is good—that one is accepted at the threshold of God no matter what color he may be.

21

When man's soul is rarified and cleansed, spiritual links are established, and from these bonds sensations felt by the heart are produced. The human heart resembleth a mirror. When this is purified human hearts are attuned and reflect one another, and thus spiritual emotions are generated.

22

God has given us eyes, that we may look about us at the world, and lay hold of whatsoever will further civilization and the arts of living. He has given us ears, that we may hear and profit by the wisdom of scholars and philosophers and arise to promote and practice it. Senses and faculties have been bestowed upon us, to be devoted to the service of the general good; so that we, distinguished above all other forms of life for perceptiveness and reason, should labor at all times and along all lines, whether the occasion be great or small, ordinary or extraordinary, until all mankind are safely gathered into the impregnable stronghold of knowledge. We should continually be establishing new bases for human happiness and creating and promoting new instrumentalities toward this end. How excellent, how honorable is man if he arises to fulfill his responsibilities; how wretched and contemptible, if he shuts his eyes to the welfare of society and wastes his precious life in pursuing his own selfish interests and personal advantages. Supreme happiness is man's, and he beholds the signs of God in the world and in the human soul, if he urges on the steed of high endeavor in the arena of civilization and justice.

23

Sincerity is the foundation-stone of faith. That is, a religious individual must disregard his personal desires and seek in whatever way he can wholeheartedly to serve the public interest; and it is impossible for a human being to turn aside from his own selfish advantages and sacrifice his own good for the good of the community except through true religious faith. For self-love is kneaded into the very clay of man, and it is not possible that, without any hope of a substantial reward, he should neglect his own present material good. That individual, however, who puts his faith in God and believes in the words of God—because he is promised and certain of a plentiful reward in the next life, and because worldly benefits as compared to the abiding joy and glory of future planes of existence are nothing to him—will for the sake of God abandon his own peace and profit and will freely consecrate his heart and soul to the common good.

24

In order to find truth we must give up our prejudices, our own small trivial notions; an open receptive mind is essential. If our chalice is full of self, there is no room in it for the water of life. The fact that we imagine ourselves to be right and everybody else wrong is the greatest of all obstacles in the path towards unity, and unity is necessary if we would reach truth, for truth is one.

Therefore it is imperative that we should renounce our own particular prejudices and superstitions if we earnestly desire to seek the truth. Unless we make a distinction in our minds between dogma, superstition and prejudice on the one hand, and truth on the other, we cannot succeed. When we are in earnest in our search for anything we look for it everywhere. This principle we must carry out in our search for truth.

25

What profit is there in agreeing that universal friendship is good, and talking of the solidarity of the human race as a grand ideal? Unless these thoughts are translated into the world of action, they are useless.

The wrong in the world continues to exist just because people talk only of their ideals, and do not strive to put them into practice. If actions took the place of words, the world's misery would very soon be changed into comfort.

SHOGHI EFFENDI

26

Self has really two meanings, or is used in two senses, in the Bahá'í writings; one is self, the identity of the individual created by God. This is the self mentioned in such passages as "he hath known God who hath known himself etc." The other self is the ego, the dark, animalistic heritage each one of us has, the lower nature that can develop into a monster of selfishness, brutality, lust and so on. It is this self we must struggle against, or this side of our natures, in order to strengthen and free the spirit within us and help it to attain perfection. The ego is the animal in us, the heritage of the flesh which is full of selfish desires. By obeying the laws of God, seeking to live the life laid down in our teachings, and prayer and struggle, we can subdue our egos. We call people "Saints" who have achieved the highest degree of mastery over their ego.

27

For the core of religious faith is that mystic feeling which unites man with God. This state of spiritual communion can be brought about and maintained by means of meditation and prayer. And this is the reason why Bahá'u'lláh has so much stressed the importance of worship. It is not sufficient for a believer merely to accept and observe the teachings. He should, in addition, cultivate the sense of spirituality which he can acquire chiefly by means of prayer. The Bahá'í Faith, like all other Divine Religions, is thus fundamentally mystic in character. Its chief goal is the development of the individual and society, through the acquisition of spiritual virtues and powers. . . . It is the soul of man which has first to be fed. And this spiritual nourishment prayer can best provide.

28

The inestimable value of religion is that when a man is vitally connected with it, through a real and living belief in it and in the Prophet Who brought it, he receives a strength greater than his own which helps him to develop his good characteristics and overcome his bad ones. The whole purpose of religion is to change not only our thoughts but our acts; when we believe in God and His Prophet and His Teachings, we are growing, even though we perhaps thought ourselves incapable of growth and change!

29

The more we search for ourselves, the less likely we are to find ourselves; and the more we search for God, and to serve our fellow-men, the more profoundly will we become acquainted with ourselves, and the more inwardly assured. This is one of the great spiritual laws of life.

30

He strongly urges you not to dwell on yourself. Each one of us, if we look into our failures, is sure to feel unworthy and despondent, and this feeling only frustrates our constructive efforts and wastes time. The thing for us to focus on is the glory of the Cause and the Power of Bahá'u'lláh which can make of a mere drop a surging sea!

31

As we suffer these misfortunes we must remember that the Prophets of God Themselves were not immune from these things which men suffer. They knew sorrow, illness and pain too. They rose above these things through Their spirits, and that is what we must try and do too, when afflicted. The troubles of this world pass, and what we have left is what we have made of our souls, so it is to this we must look to becoming more spiritual, drawing nearer to God, no matter what our human minds and bodies go through.

32

The complete and entire elimination of the ego would imply perfection—which man can never completely attain—but the ego can and should be ever-increasingly subordinated to the enlightened soul of man. This is what spiritual progress implies.

33

Each of us is responsible for one life only, and that is our own. Each of us is immeasurably far from being "perfect as our heavenly father is perfect" and the task of perfecting our own life and character is one that requires all our attention, our will-power and energy. If we allow our attention and energy to be taken up in efforts to keep others right and remedy their faults, we are wasting precious time. We are like ploughmen each of whom has his team to manage and his plough to direct, and in order to keep his furrow straight he must keep his eye on his goal and concentrate on his own task. If he looks to this side and that to see how Tom and Harry are getting on and to criticize their ploughing, then his own furrow will assuredly become crooked.

THE UNIVERSAL HOUSE
OF JUSTICE

34

You share in common with your fellow believers the unique bounty of having recognized the Supreme Manifestation of God, Bahá'u'lláh. This fact empowers you and them to engage in a necessary process of spiritual transformation, a process which is slow and sometimes can be painful. The most significant contribution one can make to the progress of such a transformation is first to deal with one's own spiritual deficiencies, then to attempt lovingly, patiently and confidently to encourage others in their strivings to adhere to the principles of the Cause. However, such encouragement is most effective not through words alone, but especially to the extent one's own "... inner life and private character mirror forth in their manifold aspects the splendor of those eternal principles proclaimed by Bahá'u'lláh."

35

Every believer needs to remember that an essential characteristic of this physical world is that we are constantly faced with trials, tribulations, hardships and sufferings and that by overcoming them we achieve our moral and spiritual development; that we must seek to accomplish in the future what we may have failed to do in the past; that this is the way God tests His servants and we should look upon every failure or shortcoming as an opportunity to try again and to acquire a fuller consciousness of the Divine Will and purpose.

The Institutions

BAHÁ'U'LLÁH

1

The Great Being saith: The heaven of divine wisdom is illumined with the two luminaries of consultation and compassion. Take ye counsel together in all matters, inasmuch as consultation is the lamp of guidance which leadeth the way, and is the bestower of understanding.

‘ABDU’L-BAHÁ

2

The prime requisites for them that take counsel together are purity of motive, radiance of spirit, detachment from all else save God, attraction to His Divine Fragrances, humility and lowliness amongst His loved ones, patience and long-suffering in difficulties and servitude to His exalted Threshold. Should they be graciously aided to acquire these attributes, victory from the unseen Kingdom of Bahá shall be vouchsafed to them.

3

They must, when coming together, turn their faces to the Kingdom on high and ask aid from the Realm of Glory. They must then proceed with the utmost devotion, courtesy, dignity, care and moderation to express their views. They must in every matter search out the truth and not insist upon their own opinion, for stubbornness and persistence in one's views will lead ultimately to discord and wrangling and the truth will remain hidden.

4

The disease which afflicts the body politic is lack of love and absence of altruism. In the hearts of men no real love is found, and the condition is such that, unless their susceptibilities are quickened by some power so that unity, love and accord may develop within them, there can be no healing, no agreement among mankind. Love and unity are the needs of the body politic today. Without these there can be no progress or prosperity attained. Therefore, the friends of God must adhere to the power which will create this love and unity in the hearts of the sons of men. Science cannot cure the illness of the body politic. Science cannot create amity and fellowship in human hearts. Neither can patriotism nor racial allegiance effect a remedy. It must be accomplished solely through the divine bounties and spiritual bestowals which have descended from God in this day for that purpose. This is an exigency of the times, and the divine remedy has been provided. The spiritual teachings of the religion of God can alone create this love, unity and accord in human hearts.

5

The primary, the most urgent requirement is the promotion of education. It is inconceivable that any nation should achieve prosperity and success unless this paramount, this fundamental concern is carried forward. The principal reason for the decline and fall of peoples is ignorance. Today the mass of the people are uninformed even as to ordinary affairs, how much less do they grasp the core of the important problems and complex needs of the time.

6

Discussions must all be confined to spiritual matters that pertain to the training of souls, the instruction of children, the relief of the poor, the help of the feeble throughout all classes in the world, kindness to all peoples, the diffusion of the fragrances of God and the exaltation of His Holy Word. Should they endeavor to fulfill these conditions the Grace of the Holy Spirit shall be vouchsafed unto them, and that assembly shall become the center of the Divine blessings, the hosts of Divine confirmation shall come to their aid, and they shall day by day receive a new effusion of Spirit.

7

So it will come to pass that when women participate fully and equally in the affairs of the world, when they enter confidently and capably the great arena of laws and politics, war will cease; for woman will be the obstacle and hindrance to it. This is true and without doubt.

8

Kings must rule with wisdom and justice; prince, peer and peasant alike have equal rights to just treatment, there must be no favor shown to individuals. A judge must be no "respecter of persons," but must administer the law with strict impartiality in every case brought before him.

9

Those persons who are selected to serve the public, or are appointed to administrative positions, should perform their duties in a spirit of true servitude and ready compliance. That is to say, they should be distinguished by their goodly disposition and virtuous character, content themselves with their allotted remuneration and act with trustworthiness in all their doings. They should keep themselves aloof from unworthy motives, and be far removed above covetous design; for rectitude, probity and righteousness are among the most potent means of attracting the grace of God and securing both the prosperity of the country and the welfare of the people.

10

Observe carefully how education and the arts of civilization bring honor, prosperity, independence and freedom to a government and its people.

11

It is evident that under present systems and conditions of government the poor are subject to the greatest need and distress while others more fortunate live in luxury and plenty far beyond their actual necessities. This inequality of portion and privilege is one of the deep and vital problems of human society. That there is need of an equalization and apportionment by which all may possess the comforts and privileges of life is evident. The remedy must be legislative readjustment of conditions. The rich too must be merciful to the poor, contributing from willing hearts to their needs without being forced or compelled to do so. The composure of the world will be assured by the establishment of this principle in the religious life of mankind.

12

There must be special laws made, dealing with these extremes of riches and of want. The members of the Government should consider the laws of God when they are framing plans for the ruling of the people. The general rights of mankind must be guarded and preserved.

The government of the countries should conform to the Divine Law which gives equal justice to all. This is the only way in which the deplorable superfluity of great wealth and miserable, demoralizing, degrading poverty can be abolished. Not until this is done will the Law of God be obeyed.

13

Oh, friends of God, be living examples of justice! So that by the Mercy of God, the world may see in your actions that you manifest the attributes of justice and mercy.

Justice is not limited, it is a universal quality. Its operation must be carried out in all classes, from the highest to the lowest. Justice must be sacred, and the rights of all the people must be considered. Desire for others only that which you desire for yourselves. Then shall we rejoice in the Sun of Justice, which shines from the Horizon of God.

SHOGHI EFFENDI

14

The plight of mankind, the condition and circumstances under which we live and labor are truly disheartening, and the darkness of prejudice and ill-will enough to chill the stoutest heart. Disillusion and dismay are invading the hearts of peoples and nations, and the hope and vision of a united and regenerated humanity is growing dimmer and dimmer every day. Time-honored institutions, cherished ideals, and sacred traditions are suffering in these days of bewildering change, from the effects of the gravest onslaught, and the precious fruit of centuries of patient and earnest labor is faced with peril. Passions, supposed to have been curbed and subdued, are now burning fiercer than ever before, and the voice of peace and good-will seems drowned amid unceasing convulsions and turmoil. What, let us ask ourselves, should be our attitude as we stand under the all-seeing eye of our vigilant Master, gazing at a sad spectacle so utterly remote from the spirit which He breathed into the world? Are we to follow in the wake of the wayward and the despairing? Are we to allow our vision of so unique, so enduring, so precious a Cause to be clouded by the stain and dust of worldly happenings, which, no matter how glittering and far-reaching in their immediate effects, are but the fleeting shadows of an imperfect world? Are we to be carried away by the flood of hollow and conflicting ideas, or are we to stand, unsubdued and unblemished, upon the everlasting rock of God's Divine Instructions? Shall we not equip ourselves with a clear and full understanding of their purpose and implications for the age we live in, and with an unconquerable resolve arise to utilize them, intelligently and with scrupulous fidelity, for the enlightenment and the promotion of the good of all mankind?

15

Let there be no mistake. The principle of the Oneness of Mankind—the pivot round which all the teachings of Bahá'u'lláh revolve—is no mere outburst of ignorant emotionalism or an expression of vague and pious hope. Its appeal is not to be merely identified with a reawakening of the spirit of brotherhood and good-will among men, nor does it aim solely at the fostering of harmonious co-operation among individual peoples and nations. Its implications are deeper, its claims greater than any which the Prophets of old were allowed to advance. Its message is applicable not only to the individual, but concerns itself primarily with the nature of those essential relationships that must bind all the states and nations as members of one human family. It does not constitute merely the enunciation of an ideal, but stands inseparably associated with an institution adequate to embody its truth, demonstrate its validity, and perpetuate its influence. It implies an organic change in the structure of present-day society, a change such as the world has not yet experienced.

16

This Administrative Order is fundamentally different from anything that any Prophet has previously established, inasmuch as Bahá'u'lláh has Himself revealed its principles, established its institutions, appointed the person to interpret His Word and conferred the necessary authority on the body designed to supplement and apply His legislative ordinances. Therein lies the secret of its strength, its fundamental distinction, and the guarantee against disintegration and schism.

17

The duties of those whom the friends have freely and conscientiously elected as their representatives are no less vital and binding than the obligations of those who have chosen them. Their function is not to dictate, but to consult, and consult not only among themselves, but as much as possible with the friends whom they represent. They must regard themselves in no other light but that of chosen instruments for a more efficient and dignified presentation of the Cause of God. They should never be led to suppose that they are the central ornaments of the body of the Cause, intrinsically superior to others in capacity or merit, and sole promoters of its teachings and principles. They should approach their task with extreme humility, and endeavor, by their open-mindedness, their high sense of justice and duty, their candor, their modesty, their entire devotion to the welfare and interests of the friends, the Cause, and humanity, to win, not only the confidence and the genuine support and respect of those whom they serve, but also their esteem and real affection. They must, at all times, avoid the spirit of exclusiveness, the atmosphere of secrecy, free themselves from a domineering attitude, and banish all forms of prejudice and passion from their deliberations.

18

For Bahá'u'lláh, we should readily recognize, has not only imbued mankind with a new and regenerating Spirit. He has not merely enunciated certain universal principles, or propounded a particular philosophy, however potent, sound and universal these may be. In addition to these He, as well as 'Abdu'l-Bahá after Him, has, unlike the Dispensations of the past, clearly and specifically laid down a set of Laws, established definite institutions, and provided for the essentials of a Divine Economy. These are destined to be a pattern for future society, a supreme instrument for the establishment of the Most Great Peace, and the one agency for the unification of the world, and the proclamation of the reign of righteousness and justice upon the earth. Not only have they revealed all the directions required for the practical realization of those ideals which the Prophets of God have visualized, and which from time immemorial have inflamed the imagination of seers and poets in every age.

19

Leaders of religion, exponents of political theories, governors of human institutions, who at present are witnessing with perplexity and dismay the bankruptcy of their ideas, and the disintegration of their handiwork, would do well to turn their gaze to the Revelation of Bahá'u'lláh, and to meditate upon the World Order which, lying enshrined in His teachings, is slowly and imperceptibly rising amid the welter and chaos of present-day civilization.

20

The call of Bahá'u'lláh is primarily directed against all forms of provincialism, all insularities and prejudices. If long-cherished ideals and time-honored institutions, if certain social assumptions and religious formulae have ceased to promote the welfare of the generality of mankind, if they no longer minister to the needs of a continually evolving humanity, let them be swept away and relegated to the limbo of obsolescent and forgotten doctrines. Why should these, in a world subject to the immutable law of change and decay, be exempt from the deterioration that must needs overtake every human institution? For legal standards, political and economic theories are solely designed to safeguard the interests of humanity as a whole, and not humanity to be crucified for the preservation of the integrity of any particular law or doctrine.

21

World unity is the goal towards which a harassed humanity is striving. Nation-building has come to an end. The anarchy inherent in state sovereignty is moving towards a climax. A world, growing to maturity, must abandon this fetish, recognize the oneness and wholeness of human relationships, and establish once for all the machinery that can best incarnate this fundamental principle of its life.

22

The world is, in truth, moving on towards its destiny. The interdependence of the peoples and nations of the earth, whatever the leaders of the divisive forces of the world may say or do, is already an accomplished fact. Its unity in the economic sphere is now understood and recognized. The welfare of the part means the welfare of the whole, and the distress of the part brings distress to the whole.

THE UNIVERSAL HOUSE
OF JUSTICE

23

Every institution of this divinely created Order is one more refuge for a distraught populace; every soul illumined by the light of the sacred Message is one more link in the oneness of mankind, one more servant ministering to the needs of an ailing world.

24

What should be stated plainly here is that Bahá'ís do not believe the transformation thus envisioned will come about exclusively through their own efforts. Nor are they trying to create a movement that would seek to impose on society their vision of the future. Every nation and every group—indeed, every individual—will, to a greater or lesser degree, contribute to the emergence of the world civilization towards which humanity is irresistibly moving. Unity will progressively be achieved, as foreshadowed by 'Abdu'l-Bahá, in different realms of social existence, for instance, "unity in the political realm," "unity of thought in world undertakings," "unity of races" and the "unity of nations."

As these come to be realized, the structures of a politically united world, which respects the full diversity of culture and provides channels for the expression of dignity and honour, will gradually take shape.

25

They are never to lose sight of the aim of the Faith to effect a transformation of society, remoulding its institutions and processes, on a scale never before witnessed. To this end, they must remain acutely aware of the inadequacies of current modes of thinking and doing—this, without feeling the least degree of superiority, without assuming an air of secrecy or aloofness, and without adopting an unnecessarily critical stance towards society.

26

The World Order of Bahá'u'lláh is the divinely ordained system for which nations and peoples so desperately search. Hailed by the Báb in the Persian Bayan, its foundational features prescribed by Bahá'u'lláh Himself, this Order is without precedent in human history for its standard of justice and its commitment to the practical realization of the oneness of mankind, as well as for its capacity to promote change and the advancement of world civilization. It provides the means by which the Divine Will illumines the path of human progress and guides the eventual establishment of the Kingdom of God on earth.

27

Every follower of Bahá'u'lláh knows well that the purpose of His Revelation is to bring into being a new creation. No sooner had "the First Call gone forth from His lips than the whole creation was revolutionized, and all that are in the heavens and all that are on earth were stirred to the depths." The individual, the institutions, and the community—the three protagonists in the Divine Plan—are being shaped under the direct influence of His Revelation, and a new conception of each, appropriate for a humanity that has come of age, is emerging. The relationships that bind them, too, are undergoing a profound transformation, bringing into the realm of existence civilization-building powers which can only be released through conformity with His decree. At a fundamental level these relationships are characterized by cooperation and reciprocity, manifestations of the interconnectedness that governs the universe.

28

Though world unity is possible—nay, inevitable—it ultimately cannot be achieved without unreserved acceptance of the oneness of humankind, described by the Guardian as "the pivot round which all the teachings of Bahá'u'lláh revolve." With what insight and eloquence did he expound upon the far-reaching implications of this cardinal principle! Plainly he saw, amidst the turbulence of world affairs, how the reality that humanity is one people must be the starting point for a new order. The vast array of relations among nations—and within them—all need to be re-envisaged in this light.

The realization of such a vision will require, sooner or later, an historic feat of statesmanship from the leaders of the world. Alas, the will to attempt this feat is still wanting. Humanity is gripped by a crisis of identity, as various peoples and groups struggle to define themselves, their place in the world, and how they should act. Without a vision of shared identity and common purpose, they fall into competing ideologies and power struggles. Seemingly countless permutations of "us" and "them" define group identities ever more narrowly and in contrast to one another. Over time, this splintering into divergent interest groups has weakened the cohesion of society itself. Rival conceptions about the primacy of a particular people are peddled to the exclusion of the truth that humanity is on a common journey in which all are protagonists.

29

The work advancing in every corner of the globe today represents the latest stage of the ongoing Bahá'í endeavour to create the nucleus of the glorious civilization enshrined in His teachings, the building of which is an enterprise of infinite complexity and scale, one that will demand centuries of exertion by humanity to bring to fruition. There are no shortcuts, no formulas. Only as effort is made to draw on insights from His Revelation, to tap into the accumulating knowledge of the human race, to apply His teachings intelligently to the life of humanity, and to consult on the questions that arise will the necessary learning occur and capacity be developed.

The Community

BAHÁ'U'LLÁH

1

Is not the object of every Revelation to effect a transformation in the whole character of mankind, a transformation that shall manifest itself both outwardly and inwardly, that shall affect both its inner life and external conditions? For if the character of mankind be not changed, the futility of God's universal Manifestations would be apparent.

2

This is the Day in which God's most excellent favors have been poured out upon men, the Day in which His most mighty grace hath been infused into all created things. It is incumbent upon all the peoples of the world to reconcile their differences, and, with perfect unity and peace, abide beneath the shadow of the Tree of His care and loving-kindness.

3

That which the Lord hath ordained as the sovereign remedy and mightiest instrument for the healing of all the world is the union of all its peoples in one universal Cause, one common Faith.

4

It is evident that nothing short of this mystic transformation could cause such spirit and behaviour, so utterly unlike their previous habits and manners, to be made manifest in the world of being. For their agitation was turned into peace, their doubt into certitude, their timidity into courage. Such is the potency of the Divine Elixir, which, swift as the twinkling of an eye, transmuteth the souls of men!

‘ABDU’L-BAHÁ

5

Now the new age is here and creation is reborn. Humanity hath taken on new life. The autumn hath gone by, and the reviving spring is here. All things are now made new.

6

The Faith of the Blessed Beauty is summoning mankind to safety and love, to amity and peace; it hath raised up its tabernacle on the heights of the earth, and directeth its call to all nations. Wherefore, O ye who are God's lovers, know ye the value of this precious Faith, obey its teachings, walk in this road that is drawn straight, and show ye this way to the people. Lift up your voices and sing out the song of the Kingdom. Spread far and wide the precepts and counsels of the loving Lord, so that this world will change into another world, and this darksome earth will be flooded with light, and the dead body of mankind will arise and live; so that every soul will ask for immortality, through the holy breaths of God.

7

Among the teachings of Bahá'u'lláh is that religious, racial, political, economic and patriotic prejudices destroy the edifice of humanity. As long as these prejudices prevail, the world of humanity will not have rest. . . .

If this prejudice and enmity are on account of religion consider that religion should be the cause of fellowship, otherwise it is fruitless. And if this prejudice be the prejudice of nationality consider that all mankind are of one nation; all have sprung from the tree of Adam, and Adam is the root of the tree. That tree is one and all these nations are like branches, while the individuals of humanity are like leaves, blossoms and fruits thereof.

8

Today, all the peoples of the world are indulging in self-interest and exert the utmost effort and endeavour to promote their own material interests. They are worshipping themselves and not the divine reality, nor the world of mankind. They seek diligently their own benefit and not the common weal. This is because they are captives of the world of nature and unaware of the divine teachings, of the bounty of the Kingdom and of the Sun of Truth.

9

Regarding reciprocity and cooperation, each member of the body politic should live in the utmost comfort and welfare because each individual member of humanity is a member of the body politic, and if one member is in distress or is afflicted with some disease, all the other members must necessarily suffer. For example, a member of the human organism is the eye. If the eye should be affected, that affliction would affect the whole nervous system. Hence, if a member of the body politic becomes afflicted, in reality, from the standpoint of sympathetic connection, all will share that affliction since this [one afflicted] is a member of the group of members, a part of the whole. Is it possible for one member or part to be in distress and the other members to be at ease? It is impossible! Hence, God has desired that in the body politic of humanity each one shall enjoy perfect welfare and comfort.

10

There is perfect brotherhood underlying humanity, for all are servants of one God and belong to one family under the protection of divine providence. The bond of fraternity exists in humanity because all are intelligent beings created in the realm of evolutionary growth. There is brotherhood potential in humanity because all inhabit this earthly globe under the one canopy of heaven. There is brotherhood natal in mankind because all are elements of one human society subject to the necessity of agreement and cooperation. There is brotherhood intended in humanity because all are waves of one sea, leaves and fruit of one tree. This is physical fellowship which ensures material happiness in the human world. The stronger it becomes, the more will mankind advance and the circle of materiality be enlarged.

The real brotherhood is spiritual, for physical brotherhood is subject to separation. The wars of the outer world of existence separate humankind, but in the eternal world of spiritual brotherhood separation is unknown.

Material or physical association is based upon earthly interests, but divine fellowship owes its existence to the breaths of the Holy Spirit. Spiritual brotherhood may be likened to the light, while the souls of humankind are as lanterns. The incandescent lamps here are many, yet the light is one.

11

I shall ask you a question: Did God create us for love or for enmity? Did He create us for peace or discord? Surely He has created us for love; therefore, we should live in accordance with His will. Do not listen to anything that is prejudiced, for self-interest prompts men to be prejudiced. They are thoughtful only of their own will and purposes. They live and move in darkness.

12

The supreme need of humanity is cooperation and reciprocity. The stronger the ties of fellowship and solidarity amongst men, the greater will be the power of constructiveness and accomplishment in all the planes of human activity. Without cooperation and reciprocal attitude the individual member of human society remains self-centered, uninspired by altruistic purposes, limited and solitary in development like the animal and plant organisms of the lower kingdoms. The lower creatures are not in need of cooperation and reciprocity. A tree can live solitary and alone, but this is impossible for man without retrogression. Therefore, every cooperative attitude and activity of human life is praiseworthy and foreintended by the will of God.

SHOGHI EFFENDI

13

When such a crisis sweeps over the world no person should hope to remain intact. We belong to an organic unit and when one part of the organism suffers all the rest of the body will feel its consequence. This is in fact the reason why Bahá'u'lláh calls our attention to the unity of mankind.

THE UNIVERSAL HOUSE
OF JUSTICE

14

Acceptance of the oneness of mankind is the first fundamental prerequisite for reorganization and administration of the world as one country, the home of humankind. Universal acceptance of this spiritual principle is essential to any successful attempt to establish world peace. It should therefore be universally proclaimed, taught in schools, and constantly asserted in every nation as preparation for the organic change in the structure of society which it implies.

15

Trust in the capacity of this generation to disentangle itself from the embroilments of a divided society. To discharge your responsibilities, you will have to show forth courage, the courage of those who cling to standards of rectitude, whose lives are characterized by purity of thought and action, and whose purpose is directed by love and indomitable faith. As you dedicate yourselves to healing the wounds with which your peoples have been afflicted, you will become invincible champions of justice.

16

At the very core of the aims of the Faith are the establishment of justice and unity in the world, the removal of prejudice and enmity from among all people, the awakening of compassion and understanding in the hearts of all men and women, and the raising of all souls to a new level of spirituality and behavior through the vitalizing influence of divine Revelation. The course set forth by Bahá'u'lláh for the attainment of these aims is the double task of simultaneously building an ideal society and perfecting the behavior of individuals. For this dual and reciprocal transformation He has not only revealed laws, principles and truths attuned to the needs of this age, but has established the very nucleus and pattern of those institutions which are to evolve into the structure of the divinely purposed world society.

17

There are certain fundamental concepts that all should bear in mind. One is the centrality of knowledge to social existence. The perpetuation of ignorance is a most grievous form of oppression; it reinforces the many walls of prejudice that stand as barriers to the realization of the oneness of humankind, at once the goal and operating principle of Bahá'u'lláh's Revelation. Access to knowledge is the right of every human being, and participation in its generation, application and diffusion a responsibility that all must shoulder in the great enterprise of building a prosperous world civilization—each individual according to his or her talents and abilities. Justice demands universal participation.

18

The community of the Most Great Name has the divine instructions and the crystal example of 'Abdu'l-Bahá to enable it to make its way from the wilderness of disunity, suspicion and estrangement into the bright sunlight of authentic fellowship, but the journey of transformation is steep and long.

19

Learning as a mode of operation requires that all assume a posture of humility, a condition in which one becomes forgetful of self, placing complete trust in God, reliant on His all-sustaining power and confident in His unfailing assistance, knowing that He, and He alone, can change the gnat into an eagle, the drop into a boundless sea. And in such a state souls labor together ceaselessly, delighting not so much in their own accomplishments but in the progress and services of others.

20

The signs of their progress are more and more apparent: . . . in the multiplying opportunities being sought and seized to offer a Bahá'í perspective on discourses prevalent in society; in the awareness of a global community that, in all its endeavours, it is hastening the emergence of divine civilization by manifesting the society-building power inherent in the Cause; indeed, in the friends' growing consciousness that their efforts to foster inner transformation, to widen the circle of unity, to collaborate with others in the field of service, to help populations take charge of their own spiritual, social, and economic development—and, through all such efforts, to bring about the betterment of the world—express the very purpose of religion itself.

21

This is not a process that some carry out on behalf of others who are passive recipients—the mere extension of a congregation and invitation to paternalism—but one in which an ever-increasing number of souls recognize and take responsibility for the transformation of humanity set in motion by Bahá'u'lláh. In an environment of love and trust born of common belief, practice, and mission, individuals of different races will have the intimate connection of heart and mind upon which mutual understanding and change depend.

22

The purpose of every Manifestation of God is to effect a transformation in both the inner life and external conditions of humanity. And this transformation naturally occurs as a growing body of people, united by the divine precepts, collectively seeks to develop spiritual capacities to contribute to a process of societal change.

23

In an environment of love and trust born of common belief, practice, and mission, individuals of different races will have the intimate connection of heart and mind upon which mutual understanding and change depend. As a result of their training and deepening, a growing number of believers will draw insights from the Writings to sensitively and effectively address issues of racial prejudice that arise within their personal lives and families, among community members, and in social settings and the workplace.

24

And it is all of us, whatever our share in this undertaking, who labor and long, strive and supplicate for the transformation of humanity, envisioned by Bahá'u'lláh, to be hastened.

25

Change is an evolutionary process requiring patience with one's self and others, loving education and the passage of time as the believers deepen their knowledge of the principles of the Faith, gradually discard long-held traditional attitudes and progressively conform their lives to the unifying teachings of the Cause.

26

The well-being of humanity is a reflection of its spiritual state, and any enduring change for the better in its material affairs requires a change in its spiritual condition. For this reason the principal concern and contribution of the followers of Bahá'u'lláh is the spiritual transformation of human society, with full confidence that by this means they are making a most valuable and most fundamental contribution to the betterment of the world and the rectification of its many problems.

27

The principle that is to infuse all facets of organized life on the planet is the oneness of humankind, the hallmark of the age of maturity. That humanity constitutes a single people is a truth that, once viewed with scepticism, claims widespread acceptance today. The rejection of deeply ingrained prejudices and a growing sense of world citizenship are among the signs of this heightened awareness. Yet, however promising the rise in collective consciousness may be, it should be seen as only the first step of a process that will take decades—nay, centuries—to unfold. For the principle of the oneness of humankind, as proclaimed by Bahá'u'lláh, asks not merely for cooperation among people and nations. It calls for a complete reconceptualization of the relationships that sustain society.

28

The Revelation of Bahá'u'lláh is concerned with the transformation of both humanity's inner life and social environment. A letter written on behalf of Shoghi Effendi describes how the social environment provides the "atmosphere" in which souls can "grow spiritually and reflect in full the light of God" shining through the Revelation. A clear sign that the society-building power of the Cause is being released . . . is that efforts are being made by a growing band of its inhabitants, inspired by the teachings of the Faith, to help improve the spiritual character and social conditions of the wider community to which they belong.

29

Humanity's crying need will not be met by a struggle among competing ambitions or by protest against one or another of the countless wrongs afflicting a desperate age. It calls, rather, for a fundamental change of consciousness, for a wholehearted embrace of Bahá'u'lláh's teaching that the time has come when each human being on earth must learn to accept responsibility for the welfare of the entire human family.

30

The global challenges now facing human-ity are a severe test of its willingness to put aside short-term self-interest and come to terms with this stark spiritual and moral reality: there is but one, interconnected human family and it shares one precious homeland. At this same moment, the followers of Bahá'u'lláh are examining anew the possibilities before them to release the society-building power of the Faith. . . . They will help to nurture, in every place, communities of common purpose that recognize the power of unity to heal, to tran-scend. Within these communities, every soul may find sanctuary, and in the friends' many endeavours for worship and praise, for educa-tion, for social transformation, for the develop-ment of communities—in all these, every soul may find room to grow and to serve. We are stirred by the promise of 'Abdu'l-Bahá: "The small shall be made great, and the powerless shall be given strength; they that are of tender age shall become the children of the Kingdom, and those that have gone astray shall be guided to their heavenly home."

31

The enkindled souls being raised up . . . gain an ever more profound understanding of Bahá'u'lláh's teachings—"the sovereign remedy for every disease"—and to apply them to the needs of their society. They are committed to the prosperity of all, recognizing that the welfare of individuals rests in the welfare of society at large. They are loyal citizens who eschew partisanship and the contest for worldly power. Instead, they are focused on transcending differences, harmonizing perspectives, and promoting the use of consultation for making decisions. They emphasize qualities and attitudes—such as trustworthiness, cooperation, and forbearance—that are building blocks of a stable social order. They champion rationality and science as essential for human progress. They advocate tolerance and understanding, and with the inherent oneness of humanity uppermost in their minds, they view everyone as a potential partner to collaborate with, and they strive to foster fellow feeling even among groups who may traditionally have been hostile to one another. They are conscious of how the forces of materialism are at work around them, and their eyes are wide open to the many injustices that persist in the world, yet they are equally clear sighted about the creative power of unity and humanity's capacity for altruism. They see the power that true religion possesses to transform hearts and overcome distrust, and so, with confidence in what the future holds, they labour to cultivate the conditions in which progress can occur.

32

Ultimately, the power to transform the world is effected by love, love originating from the relationship with the divine, love ablaze among members of a community, love extended without restriction to every human being. This divine love, ignited by the Word of God, is disseminated by enkindled souls through intimate conversations that create new susceptibilities in human hearts, open minds to moral persuasion, and loosen the hold of biased norms and social systems so that they can gradually take on a new form in keeping with the requirements of humanity's age of maturity. You are channels for this divine love; let it flow through you to all who cross your path. Infuse it into every neighborhood and social space in which you move to build capacity to canalize the society-building power of Bahá'u'lláh's Revelation. There can be no rest until the destined outcome is achieved.

NOTES

The Individual

BAHÁ'U'LLÁH

1. *Gleanings from the Writings of Bahá'u'lláh,* no. 125.6.
2. Ibid., no. 14.1.
3. *The Summons of the Lord of Hosts,* ¶111.
4. The Hidden Words, Arabic no. 40.
5. *Gleanings from the Writings of Bahá'u'lláh,* no. 77.1.
6. Ibid., no. 43.4.
7. From a Tablet translated from the Persian, at https://www.bahai.org/beliefs/universal-peace/quotations.

'ABDU'L-BAHÁ

8. *The Promulgation of Universal Peace*, pp. 265–66.

9. *The Secret of Divine Civilization*, no. 5.

10. *Paris Talks*, no. 29.10–11.

11. Ibid., no. 9.24–25.

12. *Selections from the Writings of 'Abdu'l-Bahá*, no. 216.1.

13. *Paris Talks*, no. 26.7.

14. *The Promulgation of Universal Peace*, pp. 339–40.

15. *Paris Talks*, no. 18.2.

16. Ibid., no. 35.10.

17. *Selections from the Writings of 'Abdu'l-Bahá*, no. 23.5.

18. *The Secret of Divine Civilization*, ¶108.

19. *Selections from the Writings of 'Abdu'l-Bahá*, no. 12.3.

20. *The Promulgation of Universal Peace*, p. 602.

21. *Selections from the Writings of 'Abdu'l-Bahá*, no. 70.5.

22. *The Secret of Divine Civilization*, ¶6.

23. Ibid., ¶170.

24. *Paris Talks*, no. 41.7.

25. Ibid., no. 1.9–10.

SHOGHI EFFENDI

26. Quoted in Helen Hornby, *Lights of Guidance*, no. 386.

27. *Directives from the Guardian*, p. 79.

28. Quoted in Helen Hornby, *Lights of Guidance,* no. 701.

29. Ibid., no. 391.

30. Ibid., no. 396.

31. Ibid., no. 1014.

32. "Living the Life," in *Compilation of Compilations,* p. 11.

33. From a letter dated 12 May 1925 written on behalf of Shoghi Effendi to an individual believer.

THE UNIVERSAL HOUSE OF JUSTICE

34. Letter dated 2 September 1992 written on behalf of the Universal House of Justice to an individual believer, in *Pupil of the Eye,* no. 48, at https://bahai9.com/wiki/Obligations_of_black_believers_toward_racial_unity.

35. Letter dated January 9, 1977 written on behalf of the Universal House of Justice to an individual, at https://bahai.works/Lights_of_Guidance/Homosexuality.

The Institutions

BAHÁ'U'LLÁH

1. *Tablets of Bahá'u'lláh,* "Lawh-i-Maqsúd," p. 168.

'ABDU'L-BAHÁ

2. *Selections from the Writings of 'Abdu'l-Bahá*, no. 43.1.

3. Ibid., no. 45.1.

4. *The Promulgation of Universal Peace*, p. 237.

5. *The Secret of Divine Civilization*, ¶193.

6. Quoted by Shoghi Effendi in *Bahá'í Administration*, pp. 22–23.

7. *The Promulgation of Universal Peace*, p. 186.

8. *Paris Talks*, no. 47.4.

9. Quoted in Helen Hornby, *Lights of Guidance*, no. 1474.

10. *The Secret of Divine Civilization*, ¶198.

11. *The Promulgation of Universal Peace*, p. 148.

12. *Paris Talks*, no. 46.12–13.

13. Ibid., no. 49.14–15.

SHOGHI EFFENDI

14. *Bahá'í Administration*, pp. 61–62.

15. *The World Order of Bahá'u'lláh*, pp. 42–43.

16. Ibid., p. 145.

17. *Bahá'í Administration*, p. 64.

18. *The World Order of Bahá'u'lláh*, p. 19.

19. Ibid., p. 24.

20. Ibid., p. 42.

21. Ibid., p. 202.

22. *The Promised Day Is Come*, ¶300.

THE UNIVERSAL HOUSE OF JUSTICE

23. Quoted in Helen Hornby, *Lights of Guidance,* no. 1102.

24. Letter dated 2 March 2013 from the Universal House of Justice to the Bahá'ís of Iran.

25. Letter from the Universal House of Justice dated 28 December 2010 to the Conference of the Continental Board of Counsellors.

26. Letter dated 25 March 2007 from the Universal House of Justice to the Bahá'ís of the World.

27. Letter dated 28 December 2010 to the Continental Board of Counsellors.

28. Letter dated 18 January 2019 from the Universal House of Justice to the Bahá'ís of the World.

29. 2010 Riḍván letter from the Universal House of Justice to the Bahá'ís of the World.

The Community

BAHÁ'U'LLÁH

1. The Kitáb-i-Íqán, ¶270.

2. *Gleanings from the Writings of Bahá'u'lláh,* no. 4.1.

3. *The Summons of the Lord of Hosts,* "Súriy-i-Haykal," ¶176.

4. The Kitáb-i-Íqán, ¶164.

'ABDU'L-BAHÁ

5. *Selections from the Writings of 'Abdu'l-Bahá,* no. 205.3.
6. Ibid., no. 1.6.
7. Ibid., no. 227.11–12.
8. Ibid., no. 68.3.
9. *The Promulgation of Universal Peace,* pp. 435–36.
10. Ibid., p. 179.
11. Ibid., p. 57.
12. Ibid., pp. 478–79.

SHOGHI EFFENDI

13. From a letter written on behalf of Shoghi Effendi, dated 14 April 1932, to a Bahá'í family, in Helen Hornby, *Lights of Guidance,* no. 446.

THE UNIVERSAL HOUSE OF JUSTICE

14. Universal House of Justice, "The Promise of World Peace: A Statement from the Universal House of Justice," p. 8.
15. Letter dated 27 July 2000 from the Universal House of Justice to the Friends Gathered at the Youth Congress in the Dominican Republic.
16. Letter dated 2 July 1996 from the Universal House of Justice to an individual.
17. 2010 Riḍván letter from the Universal House of Justice to the Bahá'ís of the World.

18. Letter dated 7 March 1993, written on behalf of the Universal House of Justice to an individual believer.

19. 2010 Riḍván letter from the Universal House of Justice to the Bahá'ís of the World.

20. 2016 Riḍván letter from the Universal House of Justice to the Bahá'ís of the World.

21. Letter dated 10 April 2011 written on behalf of the Universal House of Justice to an individual believer.

22. 2012 Riḍván letter from the Universal House of Justice to the Bahá'ís of the World.

23. Letter dated 10 April 2011 from the Universal House of Justice to an individual believer.

24. Letter dated 1 January 2011 from the Universal House of Justice to the Bahá'ís of the World.

25. Quoted in Helen Hornby, *Lights of Guidance,* no. 2098.

26. *Messages from the Universal House of Justice, 1986–2001,* no. 96.4.

27. Letter dated 2 March 2013 from the Universal House of Justice to the Bahá'ís of Iran.

28. Letter dated 30 December 2021 from the Universal House of Justice to the Conference of the Continental Boards of Counsellors.

29. Letter dated 24 May 2001 from the Universal House of Justice to the Believers Gathered for the Events Marking the Completion of the Projects on Mount Carmel.

30. Letter dated 4 January 2022 from the Universal House of Justice to the Bahá'ís of the World.
31. Letter dated 30 December 2021 from the Universal House of Justice to the Conference of the Continental Boards of Counsellors.
32. Letter dated July 22, 2020 from the Universal House of Justice to the Bahá'ís of the United States.

BIBLIOGRAPHY

Works of Bahá'u'lláh

Gleanings from the Writings of Bahá'u'lláh. Translated by Shoghi Effendi. Wilmette, IL: Bahá'í Publishing, 2005.

The Hidden Words. Translated by Shoghi Effendi. Wilmette, IL: Bahá'í Publishing, 2002.

The Kitáb-i-Íqán: The Book of Certitude. Translated by Shoghi Effendi. Wilmette, IL: Bahá'í Publishing, 2003.

The Proclamation of Bahá'u'lláh. Wilmette, IL: Bahá'í Publishing Trust, 1978.

The Summons of the Lord of Hosts: Tablets of Bahá'u'lláh. Wilmette, IL: Bahá'í Publishing, 2006.

Works of 'Abdu'l-Bahá

Paris Talks: Addresses Given By 'Abdu'l-Bahá in Paris in 1911. Wilmette, IL: Bahá'í Publishing, 2011.

Promulgation of Universal Peace: Talks Delivered by 'Abdu'l-Bahá during His Visit to the United States and Canada in 1912. Compiled by Howard MacNutt. Wilmette, IL: Bahá'í Publishing, 2012.

The Secret of Divine Civilization. Translated by Marzieh Gail and Ali-Kuli Khan. Wilmette, IL: Bahá'í Publishing, 2007.

Selections from the Writings of 'Abdu'l-Bahá. Compiled by the Research Department of the Universal House of Justice. Translated by a Committee at the Bahá'í World Center and Marzieh Gail. Wilmette, IL: Bahá'í Publishing, 2010.

Works of Shoghi Effendi

Bahá'í Administration. Wilmette, IL: Bahá'í Publishing Trust, 1998.

"Living the Life." Compiled by the Research Department of the Universal House of Justice, published in *Compilation of Compilations,* vol. 2, pages 1–28, 1991.

The Promised Day is Come. Wilmette, IL: Bahá'í Publishing Trust, 1993.

The World Order of Bahá'u'lláh: Selected Letters. New ed. Wilmette, IL: Bahá'í Publishing Trust, 1991.

Works of the Universal House of Justice

Messages from the Universal House of Justice, 1986– 2001: The Fourth Epoch of the Formative Age. Wilmette, IL: Bahá'í Publishing Trust, 2010.

"The Promise of World Peace: A Statement from the Universal House of Justice." October, 1985.

Bahá'í Compilations

The Compilation of Compilations: Prepared by the Universal House of Justice, 1963–1990. 2 vols. Australia: Bahá'í Publications Australia, 1991.

Lights of Guidance: A Bahá'í Reference File. Compiled by Helen Hornby. New ed. New Delhi, India: Bahá'í Publishing Trust, 1994.

Pupil of the Eye: African Americans in the World Order of Bahá'u'lláh. Compiled by Bonnie Taylor. Rivera Beach, FL: Palabra Publications, 1998.